Editor
Lorin Klistoff, M.A.

Editorial Manager
Karen J. Goldfluss, M.S. Ed.

Editor in Chief
Sharon Coan, M.S. Ed.

Illustrator
Wendy Chang

Cover Artist
Jessica Orlando

Art Coordinator
Denice Adorno

Creative Director
Elayne Roberts

Imaging
James Edward Grace

Product Manager
Phil Garcia

Publisher
Mary D. Smith, M.S. Ed.

How to Solve Word Problems

Grades 2–3

Author

Mary Bolte

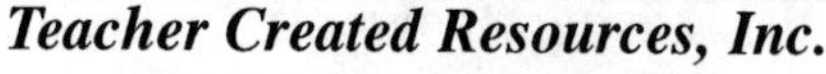

Teacher Created Resources, Inc.
6421 Industry Way
Westminster, CA 92683
www.teachercreated.com

ISBN: 978-1-57690-948-5

Reprinted, 2009

Made in U.S.A.

? ? ?

Table of Contents

How to •••••••••••••••••••••• Use This Book

A Note to Teachers and Parents

Welcome to the "How to" math series! You have chosen one of over two dozen books designed to give your children the information and practice they need to acquire important concepts in specific areas of math. The goal of the "How to" math books is to give children an extra boost as they work toward mastery of the math skills established by the National Council of Teachers of Mathematics (NCTM) and outlined in grade-level scope and sequence guidelines.

The design of this book is intended to be used by teachers or parents for a variety of purposes and needs. Each of the units contains one or more "How to" pages and two or more practice pages. The "How to" section of each unit precedes the practice pages and provides needed information such as a concept or math rule review, important terms and formulas to remember, or step-by-step guidelines necessary for using the practice pages. While most "How to" pages are written for direct use by the children, in some lower-grade level books, these pages are presented as instructional pages or direct lessons to be used by a teacher or parent prior to introducing the practice pages.

About This Book

How to Solve Word Problems: Grades 2–3 presents a comprehensive overview of word problems for students at this level. It can be used to introduce and teach basic word problems to children with little or no background in the concepts. This book can also be used in a learning center containing materials needed for each unit of instruction.

The units in this book can be used in whole-class instruction with the teacher or by a parent assisting his or her child through the book. This book also lends itself to use by a small group doing remedial or review work on word problems or for individuals and small groups engaged in enrichment or accelerated work. A teacher may want to have two tracks within his or her class with one moving at a faster pace and the other at a gradual pace appropriate to the ability or background of the children.

The word problem activities in this book will help your children learn new skills and reinforce skills already learned, as they learn how to:

- use mathematical content to explore and understand the solutions to word problems.
- create word problems from everyday situations.
- become confident in using math in a meaningful way.
- relate everyday language, pictures, and diagrams to mathematical language, symbols, and ideas.
- reflect upon and explain thinking about mathematical ideas and situations.
- use patterns to analyze mathematical situations.
- link conceptual and procedural knowledge.
- explore and apply estimation strategies.
- understand the numeration system through counting, grouping, and place-value concepts.
- develop operational sense.
- develop proficiency in basic fact computation and techniques.
- recognize and appreciate geometry in the world.
- use time measurement in everyday situations.
- apply fractions to problem situations.

If children have difficulty with a specific concept or unit within this book, review the material and allow them to redo the troublesome pages. It is preferable for children to find the work easy at first and to gradually advance to the more difficult concepts.

Standards

How to Solve Word Problems: Grades 2–3 highlights the use of various strategies and activities and emphasizes the development of proficiency in basic facts and processes for solving word problems. It provides a wide variety of instructional models and explanations for the gradual and thorough development of solving word problems. The units in this book are designed to match the suggestions of the National Council of Teachers of Mathematics (NCTM). They strongly support the learning of measurement and other processes in the context of problem solving and real-world applications. Use every opportunity to have students apply these new skills in classroom situations and at home. This will reinforce the value of the skill as well as the process.

How to Solve Word Problems: Grades 2–3 matches a number of NCTM standards, including the following main topics and specific features:

Problem Solving
Problem-solving approaches are used to investigate and understand mathematical content. Problems are formulated from everyday mathematical situations. The information is designed to develop students' confidence in using mathematics meaningfully.

Communication
Physical materials, pictures, and diagrams in the text relate to mathematical ideas. The problems reflect upon and clarify students' thinking about mathematical ideas and situations. This book also relates everyday language to mathematical language and symbols.

Reasoning
The problems include the use of models, known facts, properties, and relationships to explain thinking. The problems also require students to justify answers and solution processes. Patterns and relationships are used to analyze mathematical situations.

Estimation
Some problems explore estimation strategies and help develop students' recognition of when an estimation is appropriate.

Number Sense and Numeration
The information included in this book helps students to understand the numeration system by relating counting, grouping, and place-value concepts.

Concepts of Whole Number Operations
This book also develops meaning for the operations by modeling and discussing a rich variety of problem situations. In addition, it helps develop operational sense.

Whole Number Computation
A variety of mental computation and estimation techniques are used in this book. Questions include the selection and use of computation techniques appropriate to specific problems and determining whether the results are reasonable.

Geometry and Spatial Sense
Some mathematical problems ask for students to describe, model, draw, and classify shapes. There are also problems that encourage the recognition and appreciation of geometry in the world.

Measurement
Time measurement is used in everyday situations.

Problem Solve

Introduce the following information and examples to the children.

A *word problem* tells about related facts and then asks a question. *A fact* is information that is true. A *question* is something that is asked and needs an answer.

Steps

1. **Read** the word problem together a few times to find out the facts and the question. Look for words in the problem that may give clues about whether to add, subtract, multiply, or divide. This will help to find the answer. Some of the words follow:

Addition	Subtraction	Multiplication	Division
addends	difference	factor	group
all together	fewer	groups	how many
in all	left	how many	in all
many	many	in all	quotient
more	more	multiple	remainder
sum		product	separate
total			

2. **Name** the words that give you clues about whether to add, subtract, multiply, or divide to solve the word problem. Look at the underlined words in the problems below.

   David has 15 baseball cards. His brother gave him 15 more baseball cards. How many <u>in all</u>?

   In the football game, Anthony scored 12 points. Then he scored 18 more points. What was the <u>total</u> number of points he scored?

3. **Draw** a picture to show the solution, or use real items to solve the problem. In the example below, you could draw apples or use real ones.

   Alyssa picked 3 baskets of apples. Each basket had 14 apples. How many apples were there <u>in all</u>?

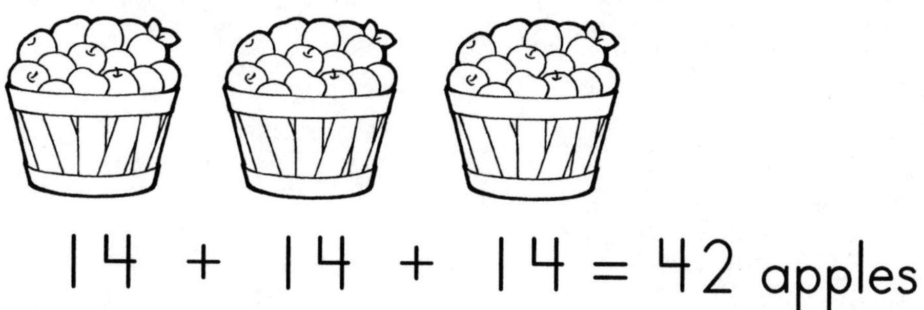

Finding Clues

Directions: Read the word problem together a few times to find out the facts and the question. Write down the word(s) in the problem that may give clues whether to add, subtract, multiply, or divide. Then write down the operation (addition, subtraction, multiplication, or division) that you would use to solve the problem. The first one is done for you.

1. The Tigers soccer team had 78 points for their first season. In their second season, the Tigers scored 89 points. How many total points did the Tigers score for both seasons?

   Key Word(s): total Operation: addition

2. The Tigers' goalie blocked 84 balls in the first season. In the second season, he blocked 92 balls. How many more kicks were blocked in the second season?

   Key Word(s): ____________ Operation: ____________

3. Nancy scored many points in each basketball game. She played in five games and scored 15 points in each game. How many points did Nancy score in all these games?

   Key Word(s): ____________ Operation: ____________

4. James scored the same number of home runs in 3 baseball games. His total number of home runs was 12. How many home runs did he score in each separate baseball game?

   Key Word(s): ____________ Operation: ____________

5. The Tigers soccer team scored 67 points in one game and 92 points in another game. What was the difference in points?

   Key Word(s): ____________ Operation: ____________

A *word problem* tells about related facts and then asks a question. Follow the steps below to solve word problems.

Steps

1. **Read** the word problem a few times.
2. **Underline** the words that give you clues about whether to add, subtract, multiply, or divide.
3. **Draw** a picture to show the solution or use real items to solve the problem.
4. **Write** the math sentence and solve the problem.

Directions: Draw a picture and write out the math sentence to solve the word problems below. The first one has been started for you.

1. Robert has three baseballs in each bag. He has two bags. How many baseballs does Robert have in all?

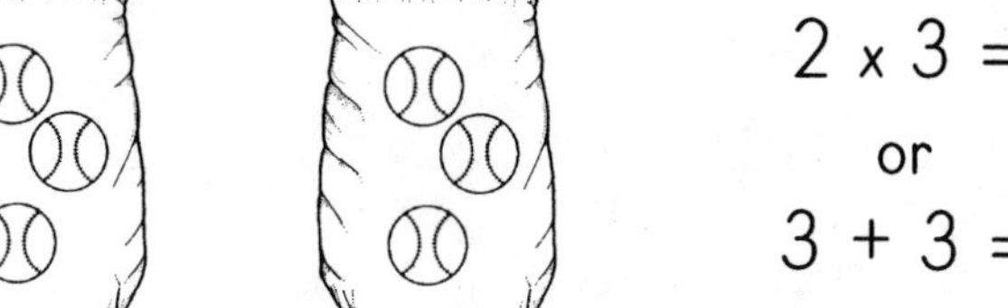

$2 \times 3 =$

or

$3 + 3 =$

2. Jackie had 19 footballs. His friends took 8 of the footballs. How many does Jackie have left?

3. The Tigers scored the following points: 9, 7, 5, 3, and 7. What was the sum of their points?

4. Susie has 21 tennis balls. She would like to give them to her friends so each has the same number of tennis balls. She has 7 friends. How many can she give to each friend?

1 Practice •••••••••••••• Creating Word Problems

Directions: Now, it is time to write your own addition, subtraction, multiplication, or division word problems about sports. Remember to write important facts and questions using the words that give clues to add, subtract, multiply, or divide. Then have a friend solve your word problems.

Addition (+)

Subtraction (–)

Multiplication (x)

Division (÷)

Communicate

Introduce the following information and examples to the children.

What does *communicate* mean? Communicate means to exchange information and ideas in different ways, such as reading, representing, listening, speaking, and writing.

Sample

Jason invited 8 friends to his birthday party.

He had 8 cups, but only 6 plates and 2 forks.

How many more plates and forks does he need?

Reading and Representing

Representing means to stand for or serve as an example of something. In the birthday word problem above, read the problem a few times. Then solve the problem by using drawings or using real cups, plates, and forks.

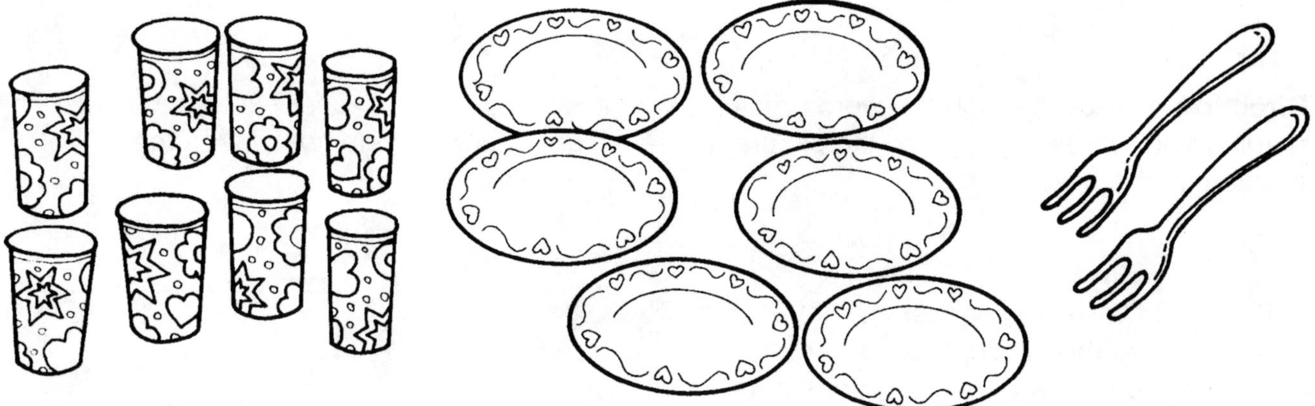

Reading, Speaking, and Listening

Speaking and *listening* is the form of communication where people talk to each other. In the birthday word problem, read the problem to a partner. Then the partner can listen and tell how the problem could be solved.

> "For the plates, count up starting from 6 to 8. That is 2. Jason would need 2 more plates. Now for the forks, count up from 2 to 8. That is 6. Jason would need 6 more forks. All together, Jason would need 2 more plates and 6 more forks."

Reading and Writing

In the birthday example, read the problem and write how to solve the problem. For example, a student might write something like the following:

> I would take 8 plates minus 6 plates which would equal 2 plates. Then I would take 8 forks minus 2 forks which would equal 6 forks. Jason would need 2 more plates and 6 more forks.

DRINK STAND

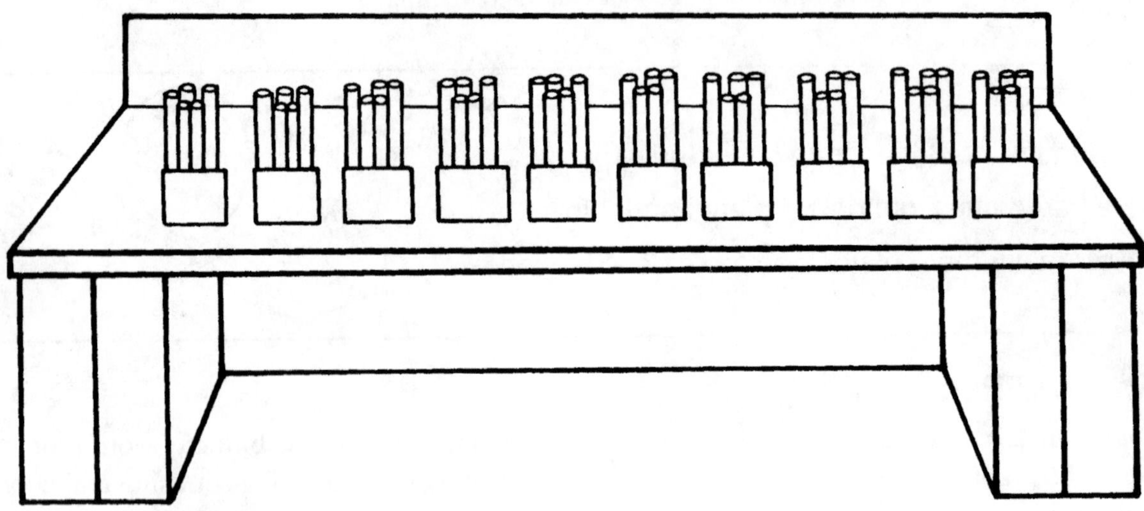

Directions: Read through the word problems about Bill and Tony's soccer experiences, using reading and representing. Use the picture above or real straws to help you. Write the answers in the boxes.

1. Bill and Tony play soccer for the Kickers. They spend a lot of time at the soccer field. After the soccer game, Bill and Tony were thirsty. So they went to the drink stand. They saw 10 small boxes of straws. Each box had 5 straws in it. How many straws were there in all?

2. Tony counted half of all the straws. What was the total number of straws Tony counted?

3. Bill needed to get straws for 15 of his teammates. How many boxes did Bill need to get? (Remember, each box has 5 straws in it.)

4. The server asked Bill and Tony to put the straws into groups of 10 to save space. How many groups of 10 did they have?

Reading, Speaking, and Listening

Directions: Read each word problem to a partner. Then have your partner explain the solution to the problem. Record the explanation.

1. Bill and Tony liked to play soccer and wanted to be on time for every game. Today's game starts at 4:30. It is now 3:55. How many minutes are there before the game begins?

   Partner's Solution: ______________________________

   ____

   ____

   ____

   ____

2. During the soccer season, Bill scored a total of 28 points. Tony scored a total of 34 points. How many more points did Tony score?

   Partner's Solution: ______________________________

   ____

   ____

   ____

   ____

3. Tony is in charge of buying shirts for the team. He spent $50.00. There are 10 people on the team. How much did each shirt cost?

   Partner's Solution: ______________________________

   ____

   ____

   ____

   ____

Directions: Examine the roundup of the Kickers' game scores. Then write three word problems using these scores. You can use the names of Bill and Tony when referring to points scored in the games. Then, in your own words, write out the solution to the problem. Share your answers with a friend.

Round-up of Kickers' Games

Game 1:	Kickers – 10	Pandas – 7	**Game 5:**	Kickers – 7	Gladiators – 7
Game 2:	Kickers – 5	Foxes – 12	**Game 6:**	Kickers – 13	Dragons – 12
Game 3:	Kickers – 8	Newts – 9	**Game 7:**	Kickers – 5	Puffins – 4
Game 4:	Kickers – 11	Lynx – 6	**Game 8:**	Kickers – 9	Ravens – 8

1. Word Problem: ____

____

____

Solution: ____

____

____

2. Word Problem: ____

____

____

Solution: ____

____

____

3. Word Problem: ____

____

____

Solution: ____

____

____

Reason

Use the following information, examples, and suggestions to guide children through the unit.

What is reasoning? To *reason* is to be able to draw conclusions from facts in a logical way. Use the activities below to review facts about properties and relationships.

Properties and Relationships

- Compare and contrast the properties and relationships of different equipment used in sports. For example, compare different kinds of balls, tennis rackets, and baseball bats.
- Observe different pairs of shoes, caps, and shirts. Discuss their properties and relationships.
- Review different geometric shapes and tell how they are alike and different.

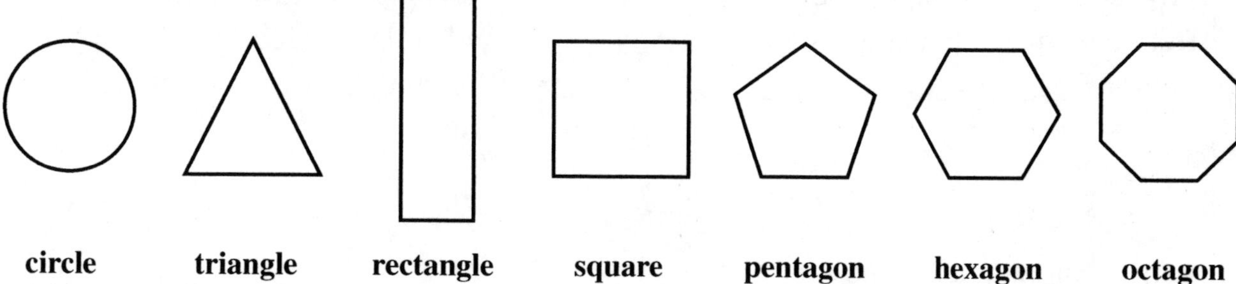

Patterns

- Use different manipulatives to form patterns and discuss their relationships.
- Review and discuss the number patterns on the baseball scoreboards below.
- Help students create various number patterns and then draw conclusions about each pattern.

Game 1

Inning	1	2	3	4	5	6	7	8	9	Final Score
Bats	2	1	3	2	1	3	2	1	3	
Owls	0	4	0	3	0	2	0	1	0	

Game 2

Inning	1	2	3	4	5	6	7	8	9	Final Score
Bats	1	3	5	3	1	3	5	3	1	
Dinos	0	2	4	0	2	4	0	2	4	

3 Practice • • • • • • • • • • Reasoning with Math Riddles

Many different-sized spheres or balls are used in sports and games. See below for examples.

golf ball

baseball

softball

soccer ball

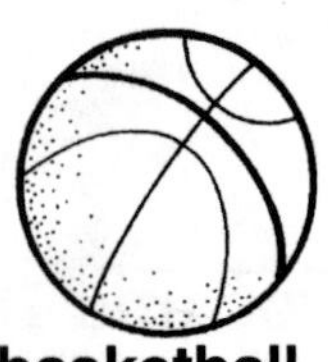
basketball

Directions: Read and solve the word problem riddles about these spheres or balls.

1. I look like another,
Who could be my big brother,
But I am smaller than my brother.
I am a ____________________.

2. I am a ball with circles,
That help me travel far,
And end with a par
That makes me a superstar!
I am a ________________.

3. I am a ball with hexagons.
And five-sided pentagons,
But do not have any octagons.
Then they would call me a "bon-bon."
I am a ________________.

4. I am the largest of all,
Sometimes found in a shopping mall.
Through a hoop I go,
And you must know that
I am a ________________.

5. You forgot a riddle about me.
I am a __________________.
(Please write a riddle about me below.)

____

____

____

____

____

3 Practice •••••• Using Patterns and Relationships

Directions: Jeff and José like to go to see their favorite baseball team, the Bulldozers, play. They made copies of the scoreboard for two of the games. Study the scoreboards and then solve the word problems.

Game 1										
Inning	**1**	**2**	**3**	**4**	**5**	**6**	**7**	**8**	**9**	**Final Score**
Bulldozers	0	1	3	0	1	3	0			
Turtles	1	2	0	1	2	0	1	2		

Game 2										
Inning	**1**	**2**	**3**	**4**	**5**	**6**	**7**	**8**	**9**	**Final Score**
Bulldozers	0	0	2	0	0	4	0	0		
Bats	2	2	1	3	2	1	4	2		

1. Jeff saw a pattern in Game 1 for the Bulldozers. Assuming the pattern continues, write their scores for the eighth and ninth innings and the final score on the scoreboard above.

2. José saw a pattern in Game 1 for the Turtles. Write their ninth inning score and their final score on the scoreboard.

3. Who won Game 1? ________________ By how many points? ________________

4. José saw another pattern in the second game for the Bulldozers. Write their score for the ninth inning and also the final score on the scoreboard.

5. Jeff saw another pattern for the Bats. Write their score for the ninth inning and also their final score on the scoreboard.

6. Who won Game 2? ________________ By how many points? ________________

3 Practice • • • • • • • • • • Scoreboard Number Patterns

Directions: Create a scoring pattern for the Bulldozers and the Blasters on the scoreboard. Then write three word problems about the scores. Share them with a partner.

Game 1										
Inning	**1**	**2**	**3**	**4**	**5**	**6**	**7**	**8**	**9**	**Final Score**
Bulldozers										
Blasters										

1. ______________________________

____

____

____

2. ______________________________

____

____

____

3. ______________________________

____

____

____

Make Connections

Introduce the information and problems below to guide students through the unit.

Conceptual and Procedural Knowledge

Math connections are links that show how math ideas are related instead of isolated. *Conceptual knowledge* is the understanding of math concepts. *Procedural knowledge* is the understanding of the steps needed to reach a conclusion or objective.

Read the story and then solve the word problems about the Woodland relay team.

Tasha and Kelly like to run. They are on their school's relay team, the Woodland Waves.

Each day they try to run three laps around the school track.

Problem 1

- **Concept:** In the first week, Kelly ran three laps on each of four days of practice. How many laps did she run the first week?
- **Procedure:** Multiply 3 (laps) x 4 (days) or add 3 + 3 + 3 + 3 to get the total number of laps that she ran.
- **Conclusion:** Kelly ran 12 laps the first week.

Problem 2

- **Concept:** In the first week, Tasha ran three laps on each of five days. How many laps did she run in the first week?
- **Procedure:** Multiply 3 (laps) x 5 (days) or add 3 + 3 + 3 + 3 + 3 to get the total number of laps that she ran.
- **Conclusion:** Tasha ran 15 laps the first week.

Problem 3

- **Concept:** In the second week, Kelly ran three laps on each of six days. How many laps did she run the second week?
- **Procedure:** Multiply 3 (laps) x 6 (days) or add 3 + 3 + 3 + 3 + 3 + 3 to get the total number of laps that she ran.
- **Conclusion:** Kelly ran 18 laps the second week.

Directions: Read and solve the word problems about the Woodland track team.

Kelly and Tasha are on the Woodland track team. They are joined by Hanna and Malia in the relay races. A relay race has teams of four runners who run and take turns passing a baton from one team runner to the next.

1. In the first 400-meter relay race, Kelly ran 100 meters in 15 seconds. Tasha ran her 100 meters in 17 seconds. Hanna ran her 100 meters in 18 seconds, and Malia ran her 100 meters in 14 seconds. What was their team's total time?

   ___________ seconds **or** ___________ minute and ___________ seconds

2. In the second 400-meter race, Kelly ran her 100 meters in 14 seconds. Tasha ran her 100 meters in 18 seconds. Hanna ran her 100 meters in 20 seconds, and Malia ran her 100 meters in 16 seconds. What was their team's total time?

   ___________ seconds **or** ___________ minute and ___________ seconds

3. In the first 800-meter relay, all the Woodland relay team scored twice their times in the first 400-meter relay race. Write the runners' total times below:

   Kelly ____________________ Tasha ____________________

   Hanna ____________________ Malia ____________________

   What was their total 800-meter relay race time? ________ minutes and _______seconds

4. The second 800-meter relay race was different. Find the team's total time.

   Kelly ran 200 meters in 2 minutes and 38 seconds.

   Tasha ran 200 meters in 2 minutes and 25 seconds.

   Hanna ran 200 meters in 2 minutes and 15 seconds.

   Malia ran 200 meters in 3 minutes and 4 seconds.

   Total: _______ minutes and _______seconds

Connecting Numbers and Shapes

Directions: Many different kinds of shirts or jerseys are worn by players in many different sports. Read the numbers in the shapes on the shirts and jerseys. Then read the word problems and draw the shapes that have the correct answers on the lines.

1. In the last football game of the year, the Jaguars beat the Tigers by a score of 49 to 45. What were the total points scored by the two teams in the game?

____

2. The two star basketball players for the Cowgirls were Cindy and Calia. Cindy scored 123 points and Calia scored 118 points. How many more points did Cindy score?

____

3. Boyd played nine holes of golf with his cousins. His score was 36. What was his average score for each hole?

____

4. Connie, Susan, Rosa, and Tamika run on a 400-meter relay track team. They each ran their 100 meters in 18 seconds. What was the team's total time in seconds?

____

5. The Robins' soccer team played six games. In each game they scored 4 points. What were their total points?

____

6. Todd likes to play baseball and hit home runs. He hit 24 home runs in eight games. What was his average for each game?

____

4 Practice •••••••••••••••• Your 400-Meter Relay

Directions: Pretend you are on a track relay team. You and three friends are on the team. Create a word problem about your team and how they place in a 400-meter relay. Share your math problem with friends.

Team's Name: ______________________

Team Members:

____

____

____

____

(picture of team shirt)

400-Meter Relay Word Problem

____

____

____

____

____

____

____

5 How to • Estimate

Introduce the following activities to prepare students for the unit.

In math, *estimation* means to make a close guess about the number, size, cost, or measurement of something. Use the activities below to help develop your estimating skills.

Number

Play the Putt-Putt game. Use a real or plastic putter to putt the ball into the hole. Follow the directions below.

1. Mark a spot on the floor for the hole or play the game outside with a real hole in the ground.
2. The player estimates how many putts it will take to make the ball go into the hole.
3. The player gets five turns to putt the ball into the hole.
4. The player discusses the completed putts and estimated putts.
5. Each player gets five chances to put the ball into the hole, and the process is repeated.
6. Discuss how number was used in estimation and why the number of completed putts was close or not close to the estimate.

Cost, Number, and Size

Buy or fill two different-sized bags with golf tees, markers, marbles, etc. The children estimate how many are in each bag. Have the students open and count how many are in each bag.

When the activity is completed, discuss how the number and sizes of the bags were used in each estimation. Then set a price for each bag and discuss which bag would be a better buy.

Measurement, Number, and Size

Fill two different-sized buckets with golf balls, Ping-Pong® balls, etc., or visit a golf driving range to complete this activity. The children estimate how many balls are in each bucket. Have the students count the balls in each bucket.

When the activity is completed, discuss how the capacity and size of each bucket were used in each estimation.

5 Practice •••••••••••••••• Estimating Golf Balls

Directions: Read the story and word problems below. Estimate the answers and write *yes* or *no* in the boxes. Explain your answer to a partner.

Boyd and Terrell like to play golf and hit balls at the Maple Meadow Driving Range. Sometimes they help the golf pro, Chris, pick up and sort the balls into the buckets. Each bucket must have 40 balls in it. Help Boyd and Chris with their job. Remember that each bucket must have exactly 40 balls.

1. Boyd and Chris picked up 133 golf balls. They had three buckets. Did they have enough golf balls to fill three buckets?

2. One sunny day, Terrell and Chris collected 220 golf balls. They had four buckets. Do they have enough golf balls to fill four buckets?

3. One rainy day, Terrell and Boyd collected 108 golf balls. They had six buckets. Did they have any empty buckets left over?

4. Boyd, Terrell, and Chris were busy one summer day. In one hour, they collected 800 balls. They had 20 buckets. Did they have any empty buckets left over?

5. Terrell worked by himself at the driving range on Monday. He had seven buckets and collected 120 balls. Did he have any empty buckets left?

5 Practice • • • • • • • • • • • Money at the Driving Range

Directions: Read the story and the word problems about golfers who visit the driving range. Estimate each answer and write *yes* or *no* on the lines. Then explain your answers in writing.

On sunny days, the Maple Meadow Driving Range is very busy. Many golfers want to practice hitting golf balls. A bucket of 40 golf balls costs $2.00.

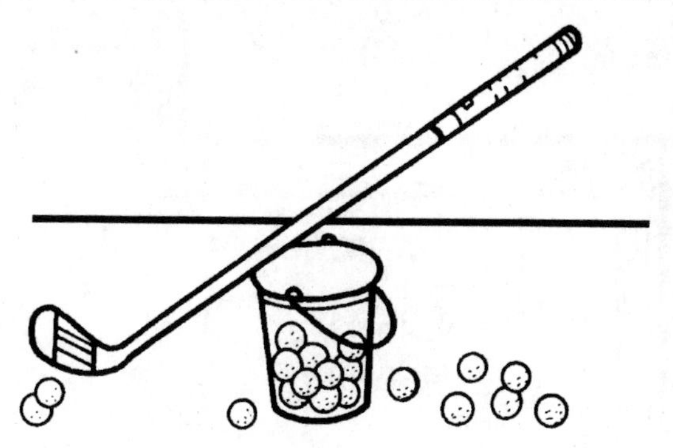

1. Mert wanted to hit one bucket of balls. She has $1.98. Does she have enough money?

   __________ Why? ______________________________________

   ____

   ____

   ____

2. Together, Bill and Alonzo have $10.05. They want five buckets of balls. Do they have enough money? __________ Why? ______________________________

   ____

   ____

   ____

3. Alia has $1.50. DiKarji has $2.00. Tony has $1.75. Together they want three buckets of balls. Do they have enough money? __________ Why? ______________________

   ____

   ____

   ____

Directions: Read the Snack Bar Menu. Then solve the word problems. First, estimate how much each order will cost. Then use a calculator or pencil and paper to compute the total cost.

SNACK BAR MENU

SANDWICHES		DRINKS		SNACKS	
hamburger	$1.12	pop	$0.75	chips	$0.60
cheeseburger	$1.46	juice	$0.64	apple	$0.38
fish	$1.24	water	$0.52	pretzels	$0.22
chicken	$1.39	milk	$0.48	popcorn	$0.56
peanut butter	$0.98			Jelly Gellies	$0.43

1. DeMarco was very hungry. He ordered one cheeseburger, one bag of chips, one apple, and a bottle of water. What was his total cost?

   Estimation: ____________________ Calculator: ____________________

2. Dion only wanted snacks and a drink. He ordered one bag of pretzels, one bag of popcorn, and a can of pop. What was his total cost?

   Estimation: ____________________ Calculator: ____________________

3. David decided he was hungry, too, so he ordered one fish sandwich, two packages of Jelly Gellies, and one bottle of water. What was his total cost?

   Estimation: ____________________ Calculator: ____________________

4. Boyd and Terrell were hungry after working in the Snack Bar. They bought one hamburger, one chicken sandwich, two cans of pop, one container of milk, two bags of popcorn, and one box of Jelly Gellies. What was their total cost?

   Estimation: ____________________ Calculator: ____________________

5. Susan walked to the Snack Bar and ordered some food. She bought one peanut butter sandwich, one juice, two bags of pretzels, and one apple. What was her total cost?

   Estimation: ____________________ Calculator: ____________________

Explore Number Sense

Introduce the following information and activities to guide children through the unit.

Number sense means to have a sense for the ways numbers are used every day. An understanding of the multiple uses of numbers in the real world enables the learner to develop meaningful number concepts.

Use the football scoreboard below to help develop number sense.

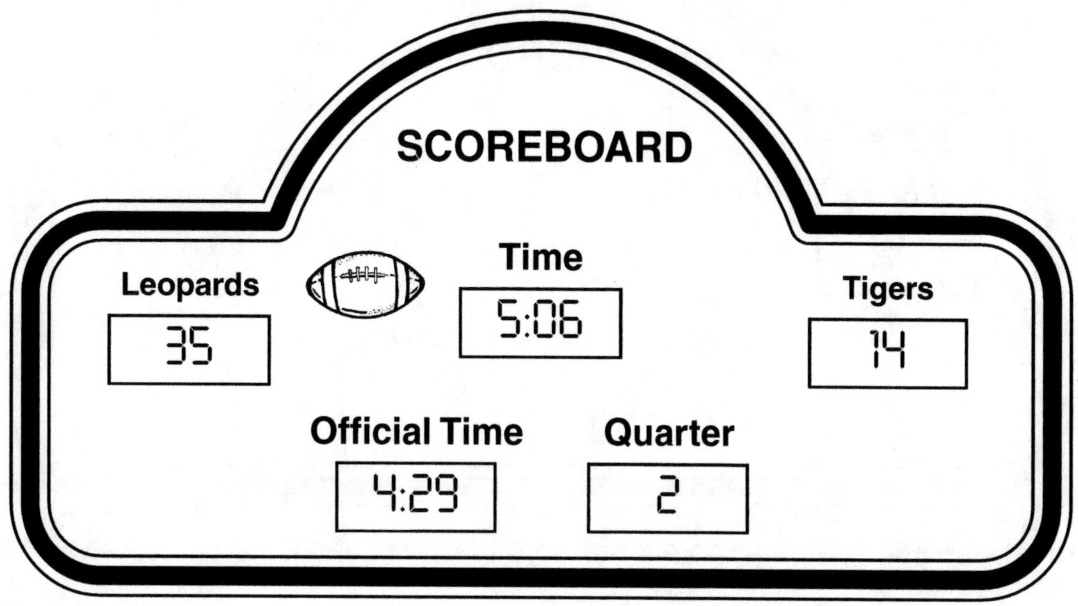

Steps

1. Look at the scoreboard. The Leopards and Tigers are the two teams playing.
2. Find the football. The football tells who has the ball. Looking at the scoreboard, one can see that the Leopards have the ball.
3. Look at the points on the scoreboard. The Leopards have 35 points, and the Tigers have 14 points.
4. In football, a touchdown is worth 6 points and the PAT (Point After Touchdown) kick is worth 1 point for a total of 7 points.
   - To figure out how many 7-pointers the Leopards have, do the following division:

     35 points (total points) ÷ 7 points = 5

   - To figure out how many 7-pointers the Tigers have, do the following division:

     14 points (total points) ÷ 7 points = 2

5. Time is also an important item to look at on the scoreboard.
   - The Time on the scoreboard is the time during a 24-hour day. The time on the above scoreboard is 5:06.
   - The Official Time is the minutes and seconds left in one quarter of the game. Each quarter is 15 minutes. The official time on the scoreboard is 4:29.
6. Each game is divided into four quarters. The scoreboard indicates that the game is being played in the second quarter.

6 Practice •••••••••••• Multiple Uses of Numbers

In the fall, Cindy and Amy go to a football game every weekend to watch their brothers—Todd, José, and Sam— play for the Wolves. They have learned to read the scoreboard and understand the meanings of the different numbers they see.

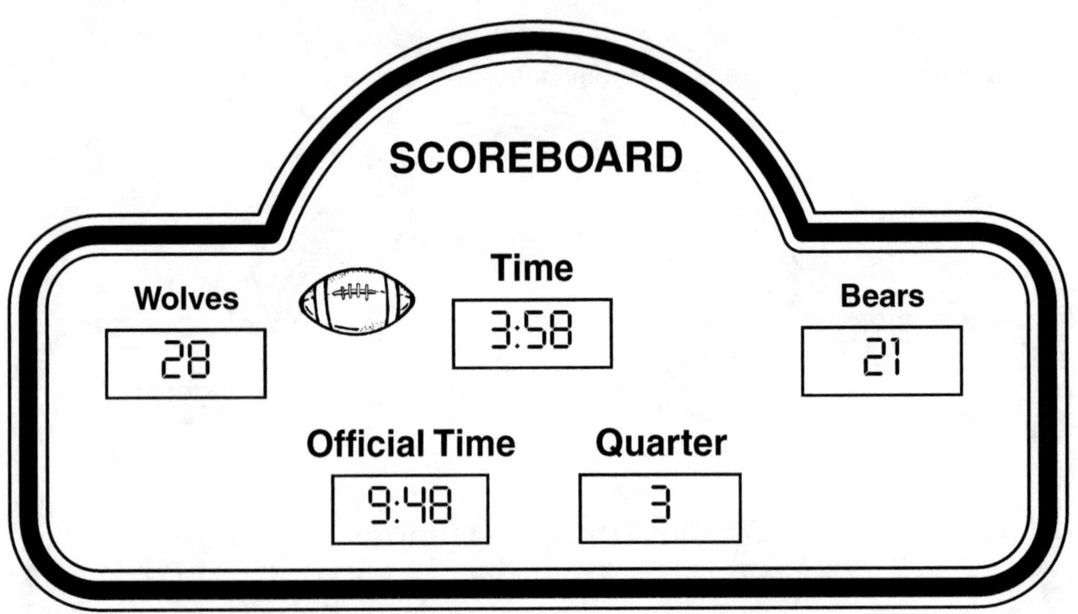

Directions: Read and solve the scoreboard word problems about the game between the Wolves and the Bears.

1. The football game is in the third quarter. Each quarter is 15 minutes. The Wolves have the ball. Look at the Official Time. How many more minutes and seconds until the end of the third quarter? ______________

2. The time on the clock is 3:58. If the game started at 2:00, how long has it been since the football game started? ______________

3. One touchdown is 6 points and the point after touchdown kick is 1 point for a total of 7 points. How many touchdowns and PAT kicks have the Wolves scored? __________ How many have the Bears scored? ______________

4. The Wolves ended up scoring 14 more points in the game. What were their total points at the end of the game? ______________

5. The Bears ended up scoring 28 more points in the game. What were their total points at the end of the game? _________________

6. Who won the game? ________________ By how many points did they win? _______

6 Practice •••••••••••••• More Uses of Numbers

At the football game, Cindy and Amy read another scoreboard that showed other uses of numbers. In football, the team with the ball gets four downs to move the ball 10 yards. If they move the ball 10 yards in four downs, they get four more downs to get 10 yards, etc. They can run with the ball, called *rushing*, or pass the ball, called *passing*.

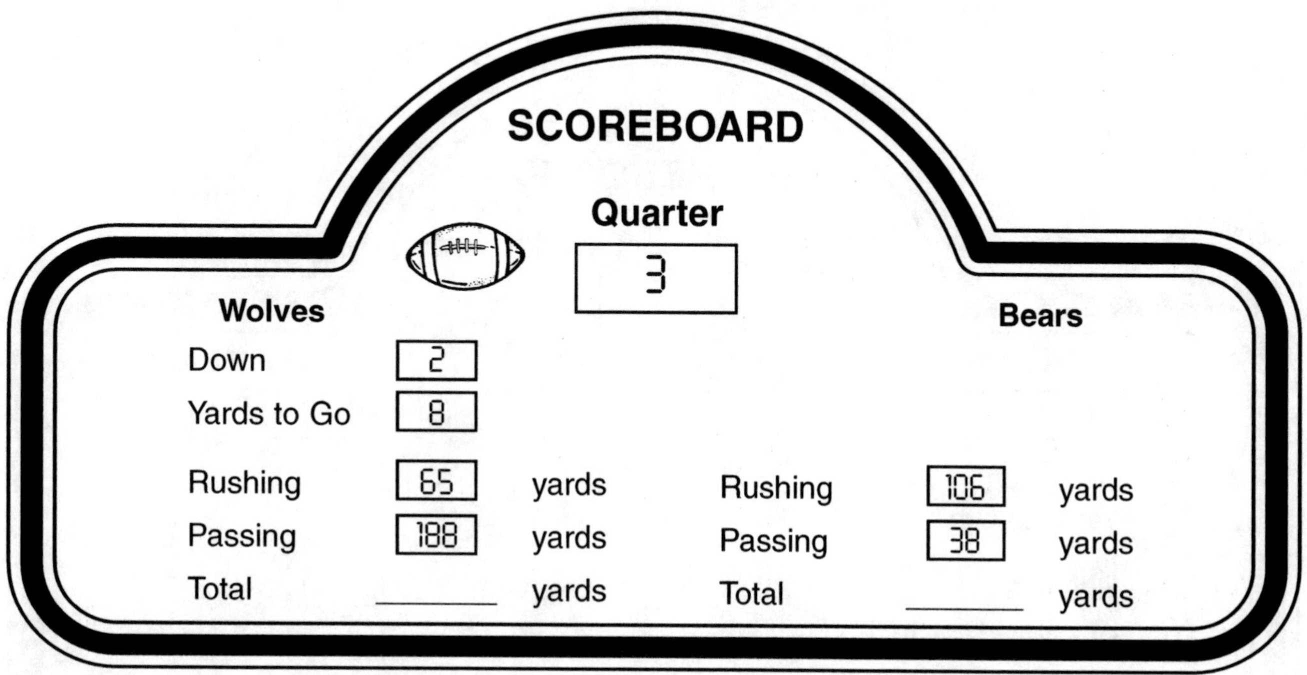

Directions: Read the scoreboard and solve the word problems below.

1. The Wolves have the ball, and it is second down. How many more downs do they have left before they must get a first down? ____________ How many more yards do they have to move to get the first down? ____________

2. The Wolves have eight more yards to move the ball. How many feet will they have moved the ball when they complete the eight yards? ____________

3. By the third quarter, the Bears had moved more yards with rushing than passing. How many more yards did they rush than pass? ____________ Were they more successful at passing or rushing? ____________

4. By the third quarter, the Wolves had moved more yards by passing than rushing. How many more yards did they pass than rush? ______________ Were they more successful at passing or rushing? ______________

5. Look at the scoreboard. Find the total of the yards that each team moved (rushing and passing) and write the number total on the scoreboard. Which team moved the most yards? ______________

6 Practice •••••••••••••••• Developing Your Own Use of Numbers

Cindy and Amy had fun watching their brothers play football. They learned a lot about numbers as they read and studied the scoreboards. Now it is your turn to complete a scoreboard. Put numbers in the blank spaces on the scoreboard. Then write and share two word problems about the numbers.

SCOREBOARD

Quarter ____ **Official Time** ____

Team ____		**Quarter** ____	**Team** ____	
Down	____			
Yards to Go	____			
Rushing	____ yards		Rushing	____ yards
Passing	____ yards		Passing	____ yards
Total	____ yards		Total	____ yards

1. ______________________________

____

____

____

2. ______________________________

____

____

____

7 How to • • • • • • • • • • • • Compute Whole Numbers

Have children refer to the following information as they complete the unit.

Computing whole numbers means to find an answer through the addition, subtraction, multiplication, and division of whole numbers. Use the activities to help select computation techniques that are appropriate to specific word problems.

Addition and Multiplication

Addition is the process of adding two or more *addends* (numbers) to find a *sum* (total).

- Use pictures to add different groups of numbers.

- Use manipulatives to add different groups of numbers.
- Use numbers to add different groups of addends.

$$\begin{array}{r} 5 \\ 5 \\ +\ 5 \\ \hline 15 \end{array} \qquad 9 + 9 + 9 = 27 \qquad \begin{array}{r} 4 \\ 4 \\ +\ 4 \\ \hline 12 \end{array}$$

Multiplication is a shorter method of adding a repeated number of *factors* (addends) to find a *product* (answer). Look at the examples below.

5 + 5 + 5 = 15	or	3 x 5 = 15	or	5 x 3 = 15
6 + 6 + 6 = 18	or	6 x 3 = 18	or	3 x 6 = 18
8 + 8 + 8 + 8 = 32	or	8 x 4 = 32	or	4 x 8 = 32

- Use pictures to add and multiply to find an answer.

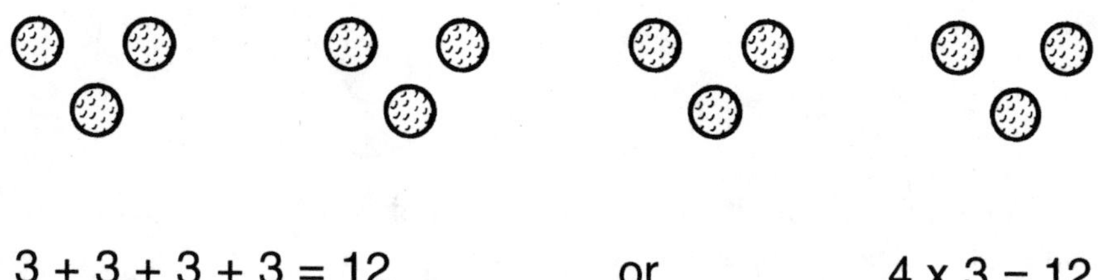

3 + 3 + 3 + 3 = 12 or 4 x 3 = 12

- Use manipulatives to form groups of a repeated number. Add and multiply them to find an answer.

Multiplication and Division

Multiplication and division are also related. Division is a process that defines how many times one number (*divisor*) is multiplied by an unknown number (*quotient*) to obtain a given quantity called the *dividend.*

Example: 12 (dividend) ÷ 4 (divisor) = 3 (quotient)

- Use pictures to multiply the groups to find a product (total).

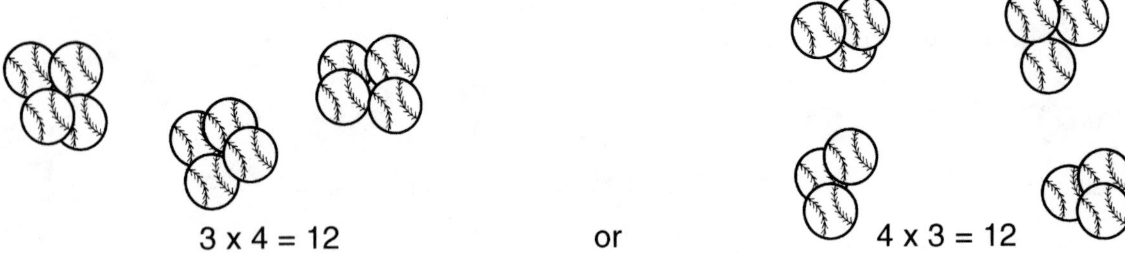

- Divide the whole group or quantity (12) into 3 equal groups to find the quotient (how many are in each group).

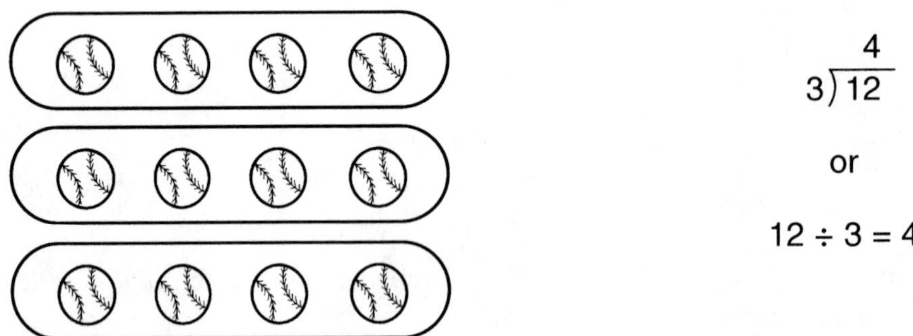

- Now divide the whole group or quantity (12) into groups of 4 to find the quotient.

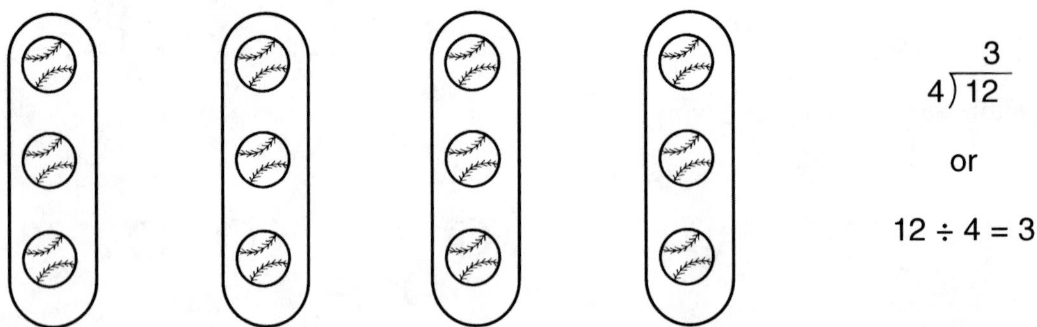

- An average is computed by dividing the dividend (a sum of a group of addends) by the divisor (the number of addends). The quotient (answer) is the average.

  John played in four games and scored a total of 12 points in field goals. What was his average for each game? 3 points

  12 (dividend) ÷ 4 (divisor) = 3 (quotient or average)

•••• Linking Addition and Multiplication

Addition and multiplication are related. **Addition** is the process of adding two or more *addends* (numbers) to find a *sum* (answer). Example: 5 + 5 + 5 = 15

Multiplication is a shorter method of adding a repeated number of *factors* (addends) to find a *product* (answer). Example: 5 x 3 = 15

Directions: Read the story below and solve the word problems. Use addition and multiplication for each problem.

Hanna and Lang play basketball for the Sunset Stars. They score many points for their team. Field goals are 2 points. Long field goals are 3 points. Free throws are 1 point.

1. Hanna completed six field goals. What was her total score?

   Solve with addition: ______________________________

   Solve with multiplication: ______________________________

2. Hanna scored seven long field goals. What was her total score?

   Solve with addition: ______________________________

   Solve with multiplication: ______________________________

3. Lang scored eight free throws. Hanna scored six free throws. What were their total points scored?

   Solve with addition: ______________________________

   Solve with multiplication: ______________________________

4. Lang scored five field goals, three long field goals, and six free throws. What were the total points she scored?

   Solve with addition: ______________________________

   Solve with multiplication: ______________________________

5. Hanna scored four long field goals, five free throws, and four field goals. What were the total points she scored?

   Solve with addition: ______________________________

   Solve with multiplication: ______________________________

7 Practice •••••••••••••••• Computing Averages

Multiplication and division are also related. **Division** is a process that defines how many times one number *(divisor)* is multiplied by an unknown number *(quotient)* to obtain a given quantity called the *dividend.*

Example: 12 (dividend) ÷ 4 (divisor) = 3 (quotient)

An **average** is computed by dividing the *dividend* (a sum of a group of addends) by the *divisor* (the number of addends). The *quotient* (answer) is the average.

Example: 28 (dividend) ÷ 4 (divisor) = 7 (quotient or average)

Directions: The coach for the Sunset Stars always calculates the averages for the team's players. This helps the coach and players to assess the ability of a player to shoot baskets. The better players have higher averages. Read and solve the word problems about averages. Field goals are two points, and long field goals are three points.

1. Hanna played in four games and scored a total of 36 points in field goals. What was her point average for each game? ____________

2. In four games, Lang scored 48 points in field goals. What was her point average for each game? ____________

3. Hanna scored 90 points in five games. They were all long field goals. What was her point average for each game? ____________

4. Lang scored 45 points in five games. They were all long field goals. What was her point average for each game? ____________

5. Who had the highest point average for field goals? ____________

   What was her average? ____________

6. Who had the highest point average for long field goals? ____________

   What was her average? ____________

7. Who had the highest point average for all the games? ____________

   What was her average? ____________

Relate Fractions and Decimals

Have children use the following information and activities as they complete the unit.

A *fraction* shows the part of a whole number or a group.

$\frac{6}{10}$ or six-tenths $\frac{8}{10}$ or eight-tenths $\frac{7}{10}$ or seven-tenths

A *decimal* is a number that shows tenths using a decimal point.

0.6 or six-tenths 0.8 or eight-tenths 0.7 or seven-tenths

Try the activities below to show how fractions and decimals are related.

- Fold a strip of paper into two equal parts. Then fold each side into five equal parts. Label each part using fractions and decimals.

$\frac{1}{10}$	$\frac{1}{10}$	$\frac{1}{10}$	$\frac{1}{10}$	$\frac{1}{10}$	$\frac{1}{10}$	$\frac{1}{10}$	$\frac{1}{10}$	$\frac{1}{10}$	$\frac{1}{10}$
0.1	0.1	0.1	0.1	0.1	0.1	0.1	0.1	0.1	0.1

- Ten dimes equal one dollar. Form a line of 10 dimes. Say and write the value of different groups of dimes using fractions and decimals.

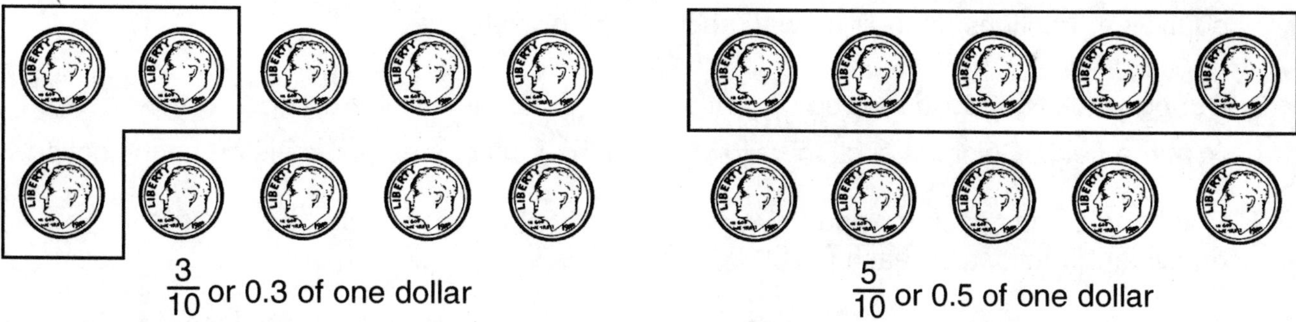

$\frac{3}{10}$ or 0.3 of one dollar $\frac{5}{10}$ or 0.5 of one dollar

- Draw picture of groups of ten objects. Then color parts of each group. Label the decimal and fractional values of the different parts.

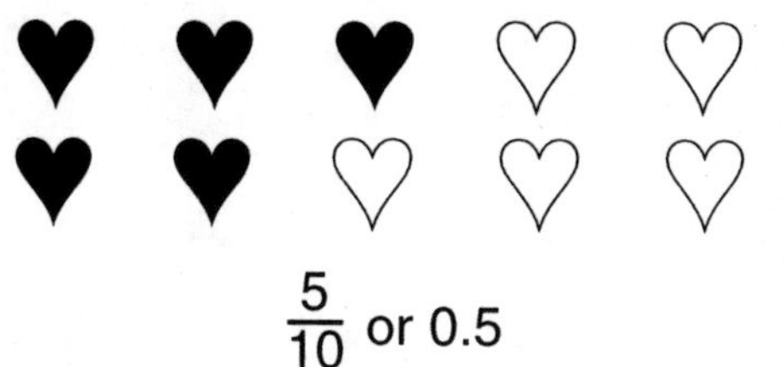

$\frac{5}{10}$ or 0.5 $\frac{3}{10}$ or 0.3

Football Fractions and Decimals

Directions: Read the story and solve the word problems.

A football field is divided into 10 parts. One part of the field can be written as the fraction $\frac{1}{10}$ or as the decimal 0.1. Carlos and Boyd mow the football field every week. They kept a chart showing the parts they each mowed for four weeks.

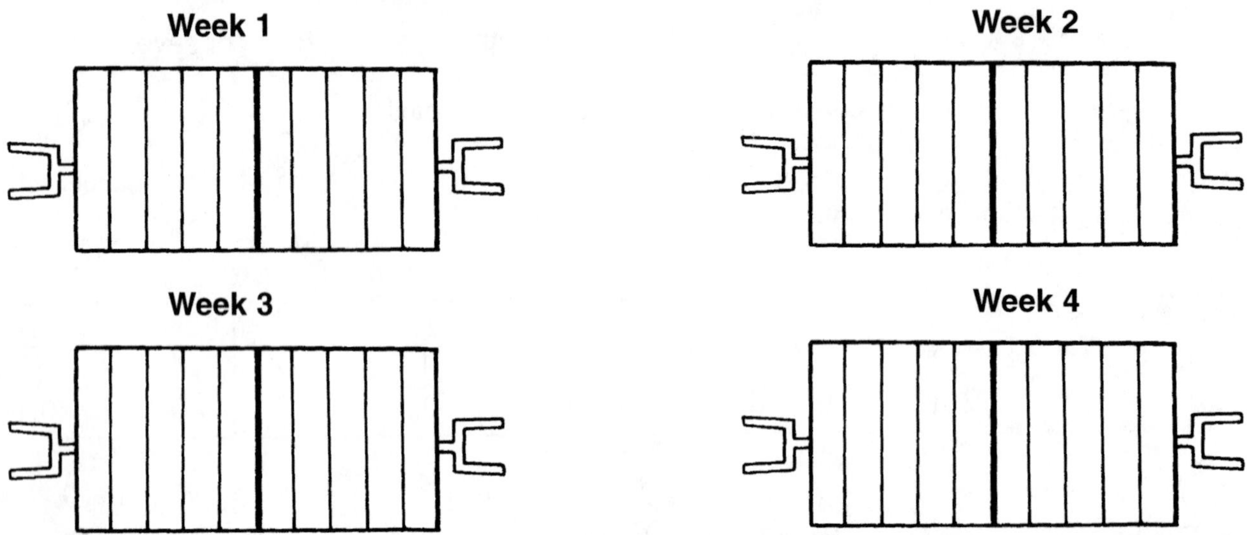

1. During week one, Boyd mowed 0.8 of the football field and Carlos mowed 0.2 of the field. Color Boyd's mowed section green and Carlos' mowed section yellow. Write the equivalent fractions on their mowed sections of the field.

2. During week two, Boyd mowed $\frac{3}{10}$ of the field. Color his section orange. Carlos mowed $\frac{7}{10}$ of the field. Color his section yellow. Write the fractions as decimals on each section.

3. Boyd and Carlos each mowed 0.5 of the football field during week three. Write the equivalent fractions on each part.

4. During week four, Carlos mowed $\frac{9}{10}$ of the football field. Boyd mowed $\frac{1}{10}$ of the field. Color Carlos' mowed section red and Boyd's section blue. Write the decimals equal to these fractions on each mowed section of the field.

5. Help Carlos write the following parts of the football field in order from the least to the greatest: 0.3, 0.7, 0.1, 0.8, 1.0, 0.2, 0.4, 0.6, 0.5, 0.9.

   ____

6. Help Boyd write the following parts of the football field in order from the least to the greatest: $\frac{10}{10}$, $\frac{2}{10}$, $\frac{7}{10}$, $\frac{9}{10}$, $\frac{4}{10}$, $\frac{1}{10}$, $\frac{3}{10}$, $\frac{8}{10}$, $\frac{6}{10}$, $\frac{5}{10}$.

   ____

Fractions and Decimals with the Fans

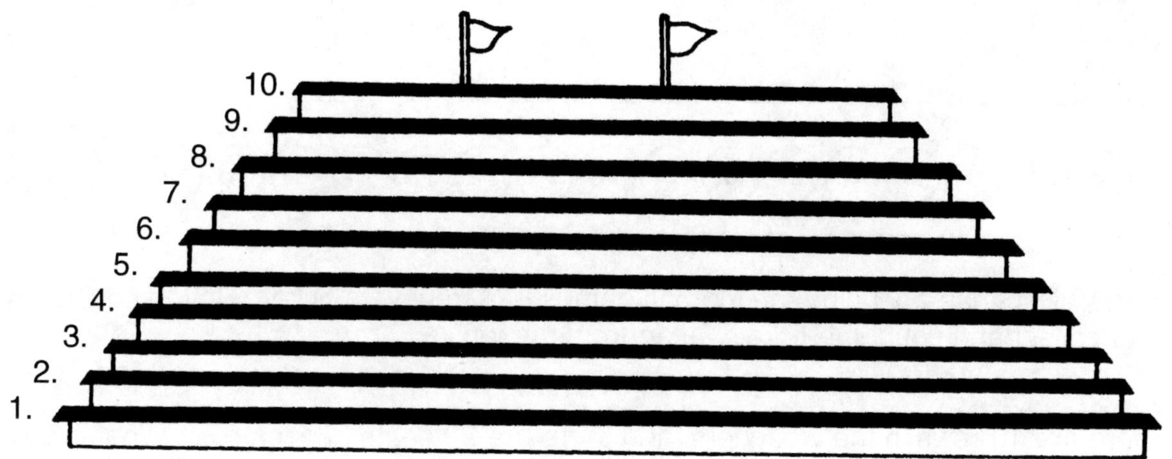

Directions: Before each game, Boyd and Carlos also help fans find their seats in the bleachers at the end of the football field. The bleachers have 10 rows of seats. Read and solve the word problems about the 10 rows of seats in the bleachers.

Game One

1. In Game One, eight rows in the bleachers were filled with fans. Write a decimal to show the number of rows filled. ______________

Game Two

2. Game Two was a night game, and the fans filled five of the rows in the bleachers. Write a decimal that shows the number of rows that were filled. ____________

Game Three

3. It rained for the third game, so $\frac{4}{10}$ of the bleachers were empty. Write a decimal that shows the number of rows filled. _______________

Game Four

4. The fourth game was played on a sunny day. Nine-tenths of the bleachers were filled with fans. How many rows were filled? _____________ Write nine-tenths as a decimal. ______________ Write as a decimal the number of rows not filled. ______________

Game Five

5. At the last game, Carlos and Boyd were very busy. All 10 rows were filled with screaming fans. After the game, the first three rows of fans ran onto the field because their team won. Write a decimal and its equivalent fraction to show how many rows of fans were still left in the bleachers. _______________

Filling the Seats with Fractions and Decimals

Seats

Row	1	2	3	4	5	6	7	8	9	10	11	12	13	14	15	16	17	18	19	20

Directions: Each fan attending the football games had to have a ticket. Boyd and Carlos helped to collect and count the tickets taken from the fans.

1. There are 10 rows in the bleachers, and there are 20 seats in each row. What is the total number of seats in the bleachers? ______________

Game One

2. In Game One, eight-tenths of the rows were filled. How many tickets did they collect from the fans? ______________

Game Two

3. Game Two, a night game, had five-tenths of the rows filled with fans. How many seats were filled? ___________ How many were not filled? ___________

Game Three

4. The fans came in slowly in the third game because it was raining. Carlos only collected 10 tickets for the first row. Write a fraction that shows what part of the row was not filled.
____

Game Four

5. Nine-tenths of the bleachers were filled for this game. How many seats were filled for Game Four? ____________ How many were empty? ______________

Game Five

6. After the victory in the fifth game, three rows of fans ran onto the field. How many fans were on the field? ______________ Write a decimal and equivalent fraction to show how many rows were empty. ______________

How to •••••••••• Process Data and Probability

Introduce the following information and activities to the children.

Students' views of mathematics and its many applications are important as they learn to collect, organize, and describe data to make predictions of the probability that something will happen.

> *Data* is information and facts.
> *Probability* is the chance that something may happen.
> *Prediction* is to tell in advance that something will happen.

Use the activities below to learn how to collect, organize, and describe data and to predict the probability that something may happen.

Data Analysis

- Review the weather forecast for a week on TV, the Internet, the radio, in the newspaper, etc., to determine if you can play outside each day. Discuss how many days you can and cannot and how you came to this conclusion.
- Conduct a survey of your friends' favorite foods. Tally and discuss the results. Which food was the most liked? Which food was the least liked?
- Observe the characteristics of different plane geometric shapes. Then tally the number of sides and different angles of the shapes. Ask the following questions:

How many had 3 sides?
How many had 4 sides?
How many had 5 sides?
How many had 6 sides?
How many had acute angles?
How many had right angles?
How many had obtuse angles?
How many had straight angles?

Probability

Statistics is information that is recorded in numbers. Statistics are used in probability, which is a process of predicting the chance that something may happen.

- Play a dice game. Roll two dice 10 times. Tally the number of pips (dots) on the dice after each roll. Which numbers appeared the most? Which numbers appeared the least? Before rolling the dice 10 more times, predict which numbers are more likely to appear. Roll the dice and then discuss the results of your prediction. This game may also be played with coins, predicting heads or tails.

9 Practice • • • • • • • • • • • • Statistics and Probability

Statistics is information that is recorded in numbers. Statistics is used in *probability*, which is a process of predicting the chance that something may happen.

Directions: Statistics and probability are very important in predicting the success of a team's performance. Read the Tygers' soccer and basketball records for their first nine soccer and basketball games. Then use the statistics to predict the tenth game scores and whether they will win or lose. Write the score and W (win), L (lose), or T (tie) next to the game number. Then write about the statistics you used for your predictions.

Tygers—Soccer		
Game 1	5 – 0	W
Game 2	3 – 4	L
Game 3	4 – 1	W
Game 4	2 – 1	W
Game 5	6 – 0	W
Game 6	2 – 2	T
Game 7	3 – 1	W
Game 8	1 – 2	L
Game 9	5 – 0	W
Game 10	________	

Tygers—Basketball		
Game 1	45 – 23	W
Game 2	37 – 30	W
Game 3	35 – 42	L
Game 4	28 – 33	L
Game 5	31 – 40	L
Game 6	27 – 26	W
Game 7	24 – 31	L
Game 8	39 – 28	W
Game 9	19 – 24	L
Game 10	________	

Soccer

____

____

____

____

Basketball

____

____

____

____

9 Practice • • • • • • • • • • • • • • • • Making a Prediction

Directions: The interpretation of data is very important in many sports, as players and teams can predict their own or their opponents' performances. Read the word problems about the players and their performances. Then make a prediction based upon the given data.

1. Tony is the quarterback for the Foxtown Foxes. He threw 10 completed passes in game one, 12 completed passes in game two, and 14 completed passes in game three. How many completed passes do you think he will throw in game four? __________ Explain your prediction.

   ____

   ____

   ____

2. Amy plays basketball for the Bryson Bearcats. She shoots many field goals at 2 points each. In her first game, she scored 14 points; the second game, 12 points; the third game, 16 points; the fourth game, 14 points; and the fifth game, 18 points. How many points do you think she will score in the sixth game? __________ Explain your prediction.

   ____

   ____

   ____

3. Leo is a pitcher for the Kona Kids and strikes out many opposing batters. In game one, he struck out 8 players; game two, 5 players; game three, 9 players; and in game four, 6 players. How many players do you think he will strike out in game five? __________ Explain your prediction.

   ____

   ____

   ____

4. Mert scores many goals for the Alexander Armadillos. In game one, she scored 5 goals; game two, 6 goals; game three, 7 goals; and in game four, 8 goals. How many goals do you think she'll score in game five? __________ Explain your prediction.

   ____

   ____

   ____

Conducting a Survey

Directions: To conduct a survey means to ask people the same question(s) and record their answers. Take a survey about your friends' favorite sports. Ask 10 or more friends the question, "What is your favorite sport?" Then record and tally the results on the graph below. Write the name of each sport on a line and color a square for each response. Then write and share two word problems about the results of your survey.

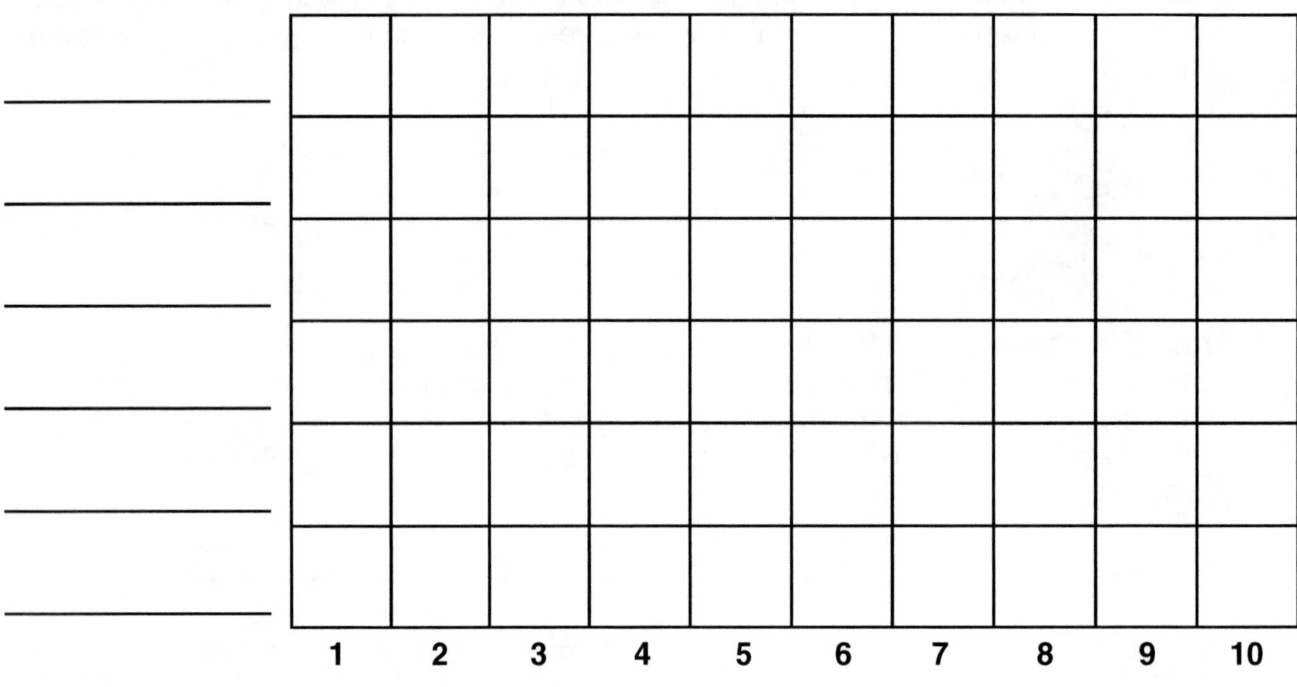

1. ____

2. ____

Sports Nuts

Directions: Matt, Brian, Jon, Neil, and Jason love sports, but each loves to play one particular sport most of all. From the three clues given, determine which sport each boy loves to play the most. Mark an **X** in each correct box.

Clues

- Matt loves baseball or hockey; Jon loves basketball or soccer; and Neil's favorite sport is neither soccer or basketball.
- Jason's favorite sport is played on the ice.
- Brian's sport is played on a court, and he hopes to become as well-known as his favorite player, Michael Jordan.

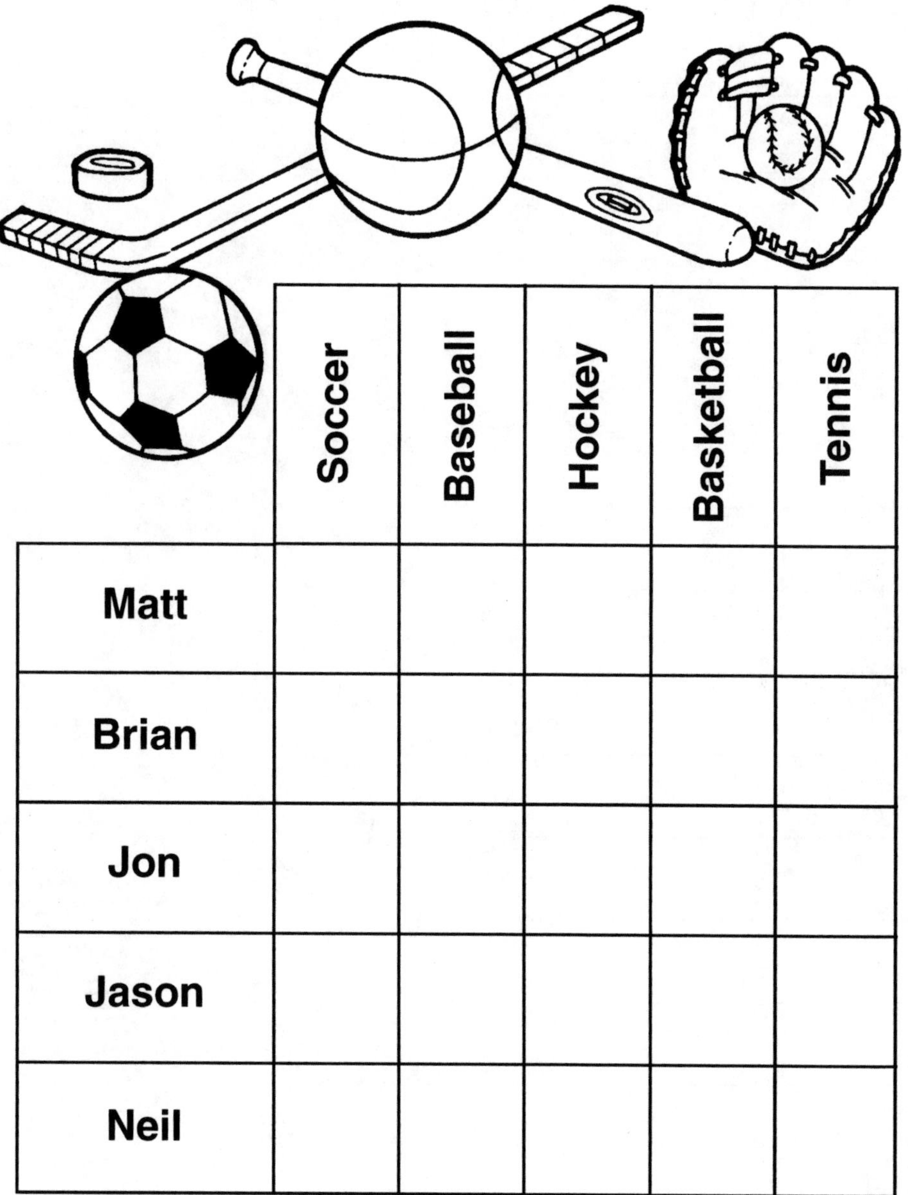

	Soccer	Baseball	Hockey	Basketball	Tennis
Matt					
Brian					
Jon					
Jason					
Neil					

10 Brain Teasers

Change for Fifty Cents

Directions: There are over 75 ways to make change for 50 cents. Work with a friend to list as many ways as you can. List the coins in order on each line, from largest to smallest. (**Hint:** Working from large to small coins will also help you find more ways to make change.) The list has been started for you. If you need more space, continue your list on the back of this paper. The first two have been done for you.

Use the following abbreviations:

hd (half dollar) **q** (quarter) **d** (dime) **n** (nickel) **p** (penny)

1. 1 hd
2. 2 q
3. ______
4. ______
5. ______
6. ______
7. ______
8. ______
9. ______
10. ______
11. ______
12. ______
13. ______
14. ______
15. ______

Riddles to Paint

Materials

- computer with paint software
- printer

Before Using the Computer

- Students should be familiar with the draw and paint tools and the stamp function in the software program and know how to print.

At the Computer

- Display a blank document in the paint software on the monitor.
- Explain to students that there are story problems to solve and that they may draw the problems with stamps or with the paint and draw tools.
- Have the students place the number one at the top of their documents.
- Ask students to draw the people described in the problem and type their answers. Students may use the stamp feature or any of the paint tools available to draw simplified pictures. Help them, if necessary.
- Read the following word problems to the children:

1. Jeff is making sandwiches for his friends. Each friend wants one sandwich. Scott and Miguel are there, and so are Pablo and Jenny. Sandra and Mark are knocking at the door. How many sandwiches should Jeff make if he is hungry, too?
2. Paula is trying to guess how many pieces of candy her teacher has in the box. Her teacher tells her that there are more than 12 but fewer than 20 and that it is an odd number. The number of pieces of candy can be grouped into three groups with no pieces left over. How many pieces of candy are in the box?
3. Lora wants to buy pizza for a party. She knows nine friends are coming. She thinks she and her friends will eat one piece each. The pizza man tells her that each pizza has 5 pieces in it. How many pizzas should Lora buy?
4. David is collecting leaves. He has a leaf with 3 points and another with 1 point. He has 2 leaves with 4 points and another with 5 points. How many points are on all the leaves together?
5. Jon and Matt each walk across a lawn covered with snow. Jon's dog comes, too, and his cat follows behind. Draw the footprints that the boys and the animals leave behind. How many footprints did the boys leave? the dog? the cat?

- Have the students print their screens of stamped and drawn objects along with the answers.
- After the children have printed the activity, ask them to use the pictures to explain how they got the answers.

Extension

- Students can create new problems for other students to solve.

Materials

- computer with Internet access

Before Using the Computer

- Students should have some experience accessing the Internet.
- Close supervision may be necessary to monitor Internet activity.

G	10	20	30	40	50	40	30	20	10	G
End Zone										End Zone
G	10	20	30	40	50	40	30	20	10	G

At the Computer

- Tell students to go to the following address:

  http://www.utexas.edu/athletics/tickets/football/stadium.html

- Tell students that a football field is 100 yards long and there are 10 yards between each line on the field.
- Have students look carefully at the drawing of the football field on this Web page. Tell them to note the following facts:

> **Football Facts**
>
> 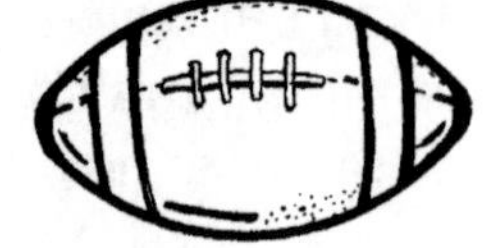
>
> Each end of the field is 50 yards long.
>
> In the middle of the field is the 50-yard line.
>
> To get a touchdown, a player has to take the ball past the 50-yard line toward the other team's 40-, 30-, 20-, and 10-yard lines and finally into the end zone.

- Ask them the following questions and have them record their answers:
  1. If you started at the 5-yard line, how many lines must you cross to get into the end zone at the other end of the field?
  2. How many yards must a player travel to get from the 20-yard line to the 50-yard line?
  3. Suppose a player catches the ball at the 10-yard line after a kickoff. How far must he run to get to the 50-yard line?
  4. Pretend two teams, the Warhawks and the Jackals, are playing on the football field. The Jackals kick off. The kickoff is caught by the Warhawks at their 20-yard line. The Warhawks' player runs hard and is tackled at his own 40-yard line. How far did the player run with the ball?
  5. The Warhawks hike the ball on their 40-yard line, and the quarterback passes the ball 20 yards. The Warhawks hike the ball again, and the quarterback passes the ball another 20 yards! The Warhawks receiver is immediately tackled. On what yard line are the Warhawks now?
- Have students share their answers with other classmates.

Extension

- Have students create their own word problems about the football field.

11 Technology •••••••••••• Painting Word Problems

Materials

- computer with paint software
- printer
- copies of page 46

Before the Computer

- The teacher should make available copies of page 46 for each student.
- Students should be familiar with solving word problems.
- Students should also be familiar with the draw and paint tools and the stamp function of the software.

At the Computer

1. Display a blank paint document.
2. Explain to students that they are going to use the paint program to draw solutions to word problems.
3. Have a student read the first problem.
4. Ask students for ideas about how to draw this problem. Any solution that includes drawing the pieces of candy and adding up the cost will work.
5. If stamps are available, allow students to use them to illustrate the solution.
6. Have students record the answers on their activity sheets.
7. Remind students that if a particular solution does not work, they can easily erase that solution and try another one on the computer. Show students how to delete drawings.
8. Allow students to work through the remainder of the problems individually. Remind them to record their answers on the activity sheet.
9. Have students print out their drawings to turn in with the activity sheet.

Extension

- Students can create new word problems to solve.

11 Technology • • • • • • • • • • • • • • Painting Word Problems

Directions: Read the word problem and draw out the solution on the computer.

1. Mia had 23¢ to spend at the candy store. She wanted to buy at least four pieces of candy. The signs in the window read:

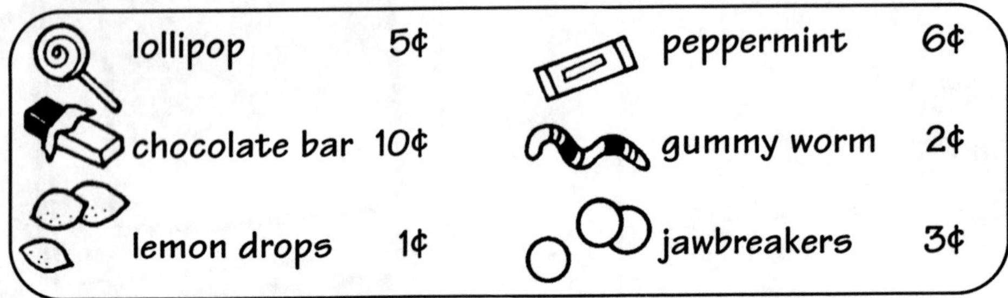

- What are the different combinations of candy Mia can buy? Draw your answers on the computer.

2. Paul and Myra went to the fruit stand with 35¢. They wanted to buy fruit for themselves and three of their friends. They found out the following information:

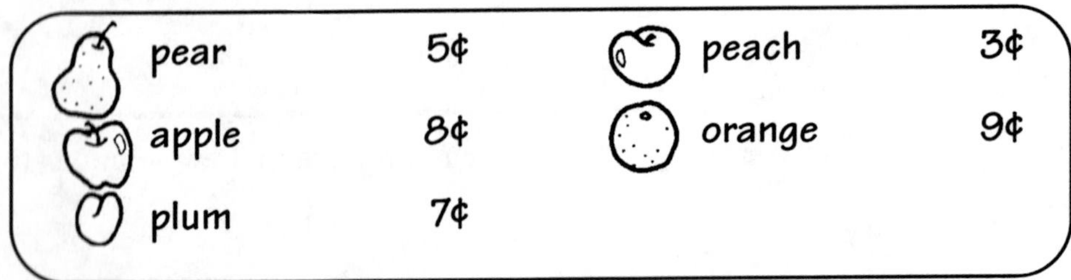

- What can Paul and Myra buy so that each person has a piece of fruit and no money is left over? Draw your answers on the computer.
- What fruit can they buy for themselves and their friends and still have money left over? Draw your answers on the computer.

3. Sarah went to the flower shop to buy flowers for her mother. She had 95¢. She wanted to buy at least six flowers to make a bouquet. Sarah found out the following information:

daisy	12¢	lily	5¢
carnation	5¢	rose	17¢
iris	12¢	baby's breath	13¢ a bunch

- … flowers can Sarah buy to make a bouquet and spend all of her money? Draw …swers on the computer.
- …rs can she buy to make a bouquet and have money left over? Draw your … the computer.

Answer Key

Page 6

1. total, addition
2. more, subtraction
3. in all, multiplication or addition
4. separate, division
5. difference, subtraction

Page 7

1. 6 baseballs
2. 11 footballs
3. 31 points
4. 3 tennis balls

Page 8

Answers will vary.

Page 10

1. 50 straws
2. 25 straws
3. 3 boxes
4. 5 groups of 10

Page 11

1. Sample answer: From 3:55 to 4:00 is 5 minutes. Then from 4:00 to 4:30 is 30 minutes. Add 5 minutes to the 30 minutes. The answer is 35. The game begins in 35 minutes.
2. Sample answer: Subtract 28 points from 34 points. The answer is 6. Tony scored 6 more points.
3. Sample answer: Divide 50 by 10. The answer is 5. Tony spent $5.00 on each shirt.

Page 12

Answers will vary.

Page 14

1. baseball
2. golf ball
3. soccer ball
4. basketball
5. softball

Page 15

1. 1, 3, 12
2. 0, 9
3. Bulldozers, 3
4. 6, 12 (or 8, 14)
5. 1, 18
6. Bats, 6 (or 4)

Page 16

Answers will vary.

Page 18

1. 64 seconds or 1 minute and 4 seconds
2. 68 seconds or 1 minute and 8 seconds
3. Kelly–30 seconds, Tasha–34 seconds, Hanna–36 seconds, Malia–28 seconds, Total: 128 seconds or 2 minutes and 8 seconds
4. 10 minutes 22 seconds

Page 19

1. 94—rectangle
2. 5—circle
3. 4—triangle
4. 72—hexagon
5. 24—square
6. 3—pentagon

Page 20

Answers will vary.

Page 22

1. yes
2. yes
3. yes
4. no
5. yes

Page 23

1. no (Sample explanation: Each bucket costs $2.00. She needs two more cents to have two dollars.)
2. yes (Sample explanation: Five buckets times $2.00 is $10.00. Bill and Alonzo have $10.00 plus five cents left over.)
3. no (Sample explanation: Three buckets times $2.00 is $6.00. They only have $5.25 all together.)

Page 24

1. Estimation: Answers will vary. Calculator: $2.96
2. Estimation: Answers will vary. Calculator: $1.53
3. Estimation: Answers will vary. Calculator: $2.62
4. Estimation: Answers will vary. Calculator: $6.04
5. Estimation: Answers will vary. Calculator: $2.44

Page 26

1. 5 minutes 12 seconds
2. 1 hour 58 minutes
3. 4, 3
4. 42 points
5. 49 points
6. Bears, 7 points

Page 27

1. 2, 8
2. 24 feet
3. 68, rushing
4. 123, passing
5. Wolves, 253; Bears, 144; Wolves

Page 28

Answers will vary.

Page 31

1. 2 + 2 + 2 + 2 + 2 + 2 = 12
   2 x 6 = 12 or 6 x 2 = 12
2. 3 + 3 + 3 + 3 + 3 + 3 + 3 = 21
   3 x 7 = 21 or 7 x 3 = 21
3. 1 + 1 + 1 + 1 + 1 + 1 + 1 + 1 +1 + 1 + 1 + 1 + 1 + 1 = 14 or 8 + 6 = 14
   1 x 14 = 14
4. 2 + 2 + 2 + 2 + 2 + 3 + 3 + 3 +1 + 1 + 1 + 1 + 1 + 1 = 25
   (2 x 5) + (3 x 3) + (1 x 6) = 25
5. 3 + 3 + 3 + 3 + 1 + 1 + 1 + 1 + 1 + 2 + 2 + 2 + 2 = 25
   (3 x 4) + (1 x 5) + (2 x 4) = 25

Page 32

1. 9
2. 12
3. 18
4. 9
5. Lang, 12
6. Hanna, 18
7. Hanna, 14

Page 34

1.

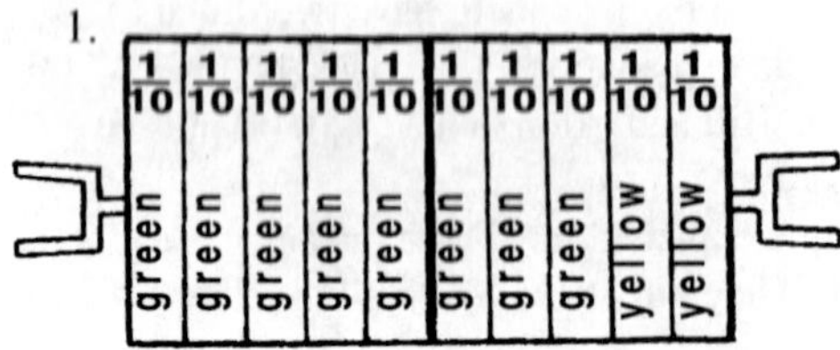

2.

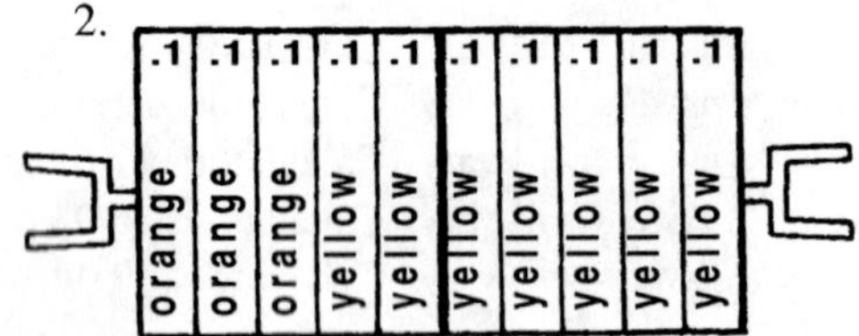

3.

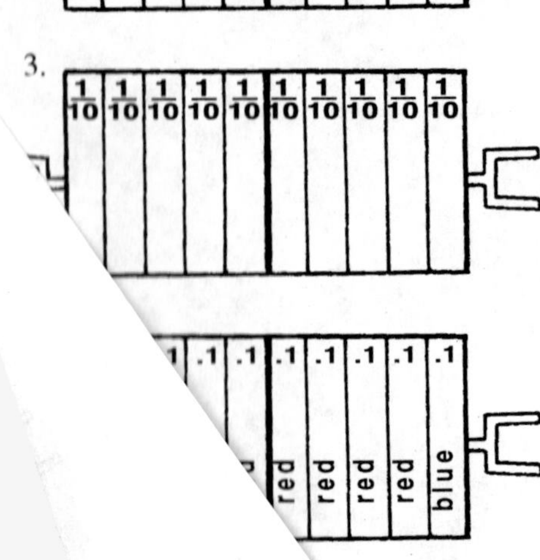

0.6, 0.7, 0.8, 0.9, 1.0

6. 1/10, 2/10, 3/10, 4/10, 5/10, 6/10, 7/10, 8/10, 9/10, 10/10

Page 35

1. 0.8
2. 0.5
3. 0.6
4. 9, 0.9, 0.1
5. 0.7, 7/10

Page 36

1. 200
2. 160
3. 100, 100
4. 10/20 or 1/2
5. 180, 20
6. 60, .3, 3/10

Page 38

Answers will vary.

Page 39

1. 16, Answers will vary.
2. 16, Answers will vary.
3. 10, Answers will vary.
4. 9, Answers will vary.

Page 40

Answers will vary.

Page 41

Matt—baseball, Brian—basketball, Jon—soccer, Jason—hockey, Neil—tennis

Pages 42

Answers will vary.

Pages 43

1. 7 sandwiches
2. 15 pieces of candy
3. 2 pizzas
4. 17 points
5. boys–4, dog–4, cat–4

Pages 44

1. 10
2. 30 yards
3. 40 yards
4. 20 yards
5. the Jackal's 20-yard line

Page 46

Answers will vary.

ades 2–3